Being a Disciple for Christ in your leisure

408

This clear, simple and balanced approach to enjoying work, rest and play will be very helpful if you've ever struggled to balance work and leisure. It is a bonus to read that Graham Beynon uses some of his leisure time to enjoy glorifying God in his five-a-side team!

Graham Daniels
Christians in Sport

A thought provoking book, the relevance of which will cause every reader to shift the balance of their rest time one way or another. I for one will be re-addressing my attitude to rest.

Debbie Flood
Olympic Medalist with Team GB

Jesus@Leisure
Being a Disciple for Christ in your leisure

Graham Beynon

First published in 2009 by Authentic Media
9 Holdom Avenue, Bletchley, Milton Keynes, Bucks, MK1 1QR, UK
1820 Jet Stream Drive, Colorado Springs, CO 80921, USA
OM Authentic Media, Medchal Road, Jeedimetla Village,
Secunderabad 500 055, A.P., India

www.authenticmedia.co.uk

Authentic Media is a division of IBS-STL U.K., limited by
guarantee, with its Registered Office at Kingstown Broadway,
Carlisle, Cumbria CA3 0HA. Registered in England & Wales No.
1216232. Registered charity 270162

British Library Cataloguing in Publication Data
A catalogue record for this book is available from the British Library

ISBN: 978-1-85078-842-3

Print Management by Adare
Printed in Great Britain by J. F. Print, Sparkford

Contents

Introduction 9

1. The anatomy of leisure 11

2. Reasons to rest 18

3. Can I enjoy myself? 27

4. Life with leisure 35

Further reading 44

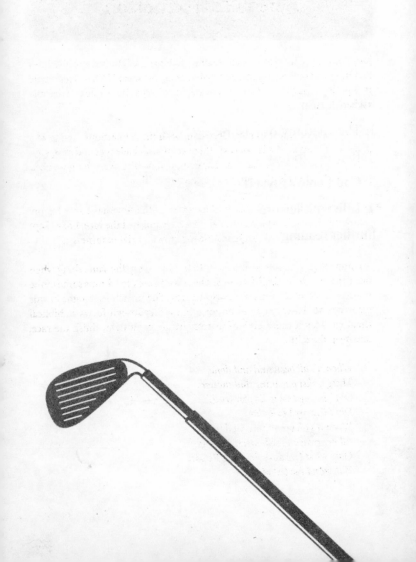

Series Introduction

Jesus was supremely concerned that his followers might be both disciples and disciple makers. But in reality what does this mean? What does a true disciple look like? What does a true disciple do? What is the role of a disciple maker?

This series is designed to help Christians with those questions. Living as a disciple of Jesus Christ is not easy; there are many challenges and struggles. However, we do believe that God has equipped us with everything we need to live a life which is pleasing and honouring to him.

In 2 Timothy 4:6-7 Paul was able to write: '…the time has come for my departure. I have fought the good fight, I have finished the race, I have kept the faith. Now there is in store for me the crown of righteousness…'

We hope that this series will help us to be able to say the same thing when our departure from this life looms. These books seek to address some of the main issues that a Christian disciple faces. The principles taught in this series are not based on good notions, but rather straightforward, biblical theology. May it cause each of us to fight the good fight, finish the race, and keep the faith.

When it's all been said and done
There is just one thing that matters
Did I do my best to live for truth
Did I live my life for You
When it's all been said and done
All my treasures will mean nothing
Only what I've done for love's Reward
Will stand the test of time

Lord Your mercy is so great
That You look beyond our Weakness
And find purest gold in miry clay
Making sinners into saints

I will always sing Your praise
Here on earth and ever after
For You've shown me Heaven's my
True home
When it's all been said and done
You're my life when life is gone
Lord I'll live my life for You

Words and Music by Jim Cowan
© 1999 Integrity's Hosanna! Music

Introduction

Our leisure, even our play, is a matter of serious concern. There is no neutral ground in the universe; every square inch, every split second, is claimed by God and counter claimed by Satan ... It is a serious matter to choose wholesome recreations. C.S. Lewis[i]

You can't really argue with this quote from C.S. Lewis. There is no neutral area of life for the Christian because we want (or at least we should want) to honour God in all of life. Our time off work is not time off from loving God and worshipping him. And we can be sure that Satan will most certainly tempt us away from honouring God whenever he can. And so we can't argue with it.

However, when I first read that quote I was struck by it – perhaps you were as well. The reason? I expect it is because as Christians we rarely think about leisure as an area we need to consider. We never do a Bible study on it; and never hear a sermon on it. (They do exist actually, but they are rare.)

What we tend to do is assume we should probably have time off from work, and we can do with this time whatever takes our fancy. So we may relax on an evening in front of the TV or with a computer game; at the weekend we may go for a walk, play some sport, do a bit of gardening, watch a film, whatever. Sometimes we might consider whether a certain hobby or holiday is too expensive or extravagant, but that is the extent of our reflection on the topic.

We need to think again. We need to think about how we should approach leisure as a topic – is it something Christians should do? If so in what way? To what purpose? With what attitude? Is it a good thing in itself to be enjoyed, or just a necessary thing so we can go back to work? Are there limits on how much I should do it or what is allowed? Is there such a thing as good leisure as opposed to bad leisure, and if so what is the difference?

If we don't think through questions like these then it is easy to see what will happen. As Lewis observed, Satan will claim that territory of life and we won't even notice. He'll grab whatever areas of life we're happy to give him – if that's our attitude to TV, sport and art, then so be it, he's not fussy. To put it differently, if we don't think this through we will conform to the pattern of the world around us and fail to worship God in all of life.

The material in this booklet comes from some sermons and seminars I have given on the topic. In developing that material I have drawn greatly on the thinking of others, and through sharing and presenting it my understanding has been refined as a result of many discussions. Grateful thanks are due to all those who have helped me in this. They have sharpened my thinking and brought insight where there was confusion. Particularly thanks goes to Dan Hames who helpfully commented on a draft version of this material. All the weaknesses are of course my own.

1

The anatomy of leisure

Defining leisure

What is leisure? Defining it is harder work than you might expect. Say the word to someone and they might think of a lazy afternoon sitting in the garden reading the paper, while someone else thinks of working on the garden. But presumably not if their job is that of a gardener! One person's work can be another person's leisure.

A party in the evening could be work or leisure depending on why you are there. Going shopping or doing DIY might feel like work or leisure depending on how much time you have and what your mood is. How do you classify having coffee with a friend while looking after the kids? For me that's leisure, but less so for my wife! What about if you find working life less stressful than time off? A friend of mine with several young children jokes about going to work for a break.

This all shows what a tricky area this is. However, despite all the complications, we probably have a pretty good idea of what we mean by 'leisure'. Here are some attempts at definitions to help us:

  • Leisure is time or opportunity for ease, relaxation or hobbies.

  • Leisure is activity chosen in relative freedom for its qualities of satisfaction.

  • Leisure is activity apart from the obligations of work, family and society to which the individual turns at will – either for relaxation, diversion or broadening his knowledge.

The bottom line is that leisure is what we do simply because we want to. It is not what we have to do and happen to enjoy, but time where we are free and choose to do something. It is therefore something that is intrinsically relaxing, enjoyable, stimulating and satisfying.

It should also be clear that it involves an activity of some kind – leisure is not doing 'nothing'. It is therefore different to idleness. The range of leisure activities is huge: reading; listening to or making music; walking; playing or watching sport; hobbies and crafts of all kinds; entertainment – including watching TV, listening to the radio, going to the cinema, plays and concerts; socializing with friends or family, either at home or going out for a meal or drinks.

This is all very well, but what about some of the complications we noted above? What about cutting the grass or doing the ironing? It has to be done but some people might find it relaxing, so does it qualify as leisure? What about the fact that home life can be stressful even when it is time off 'work'? This is where it can be helpful to think of a spectrum, which is illustrated below.

The work–leisure spectrum

Work Oligation Necessity	Semi-work	Semi-leisure	Leisure Freedom

On the left is work which is obligatory and needs to be done. By contrast leisure at the opposite end is a matter of freedom and choice – there is nothing necessary about it. But in between are areas we might call semi-work and semi-leisure. They are things with some degree of necessity but which may have some degree of enjoyment to them. What qualifies in which category depends on your interests. Things like cutting the grass, cleaning the house, going shopping and so on need to be done – at least to some extent. To some people they are semi-work while to others it is semi-leisure. Or it might depend what mood you are in and how much free time you have!

Our topic is what goes on the right of this spectrum. What would we choose to do, given the choice, with a spare evening or Saturday afternoon?

Leisure today

There are a variety of attitudes to leisure around today. We can divide them into two broad categories. First there is worship of leisure. This is where life revolves around specific leisure activities or around leisure itself. You work only for the weekend and the fun you'll be able to have. Your spare time is focused on a specific activity, whether it's gardening or computer games. We talk for example of a 'sports fanatic'. What we mean is that sport has become the focus of their life.

This living for leisure is everywhere. We can see it in the adverts – whether they are for holidays, DIY, or computer games – we should give ourselves to some leisure activity because it is what will bring fulfilment in life.

One specific example of this worship of leisure is hedonism. This is where a person lives for pleasure, but gets their pleasure from certain activities. It might be lounging by the pool or it might be extreme sports – whatever it is that will maximize enjoyment and pleasure.

Another example is leisure as escapism. People think of their leisure activities as a way to get away from the rest of life. It is usually escaping something to do with their work – that might be the boredom of work or the high pressures of work. But it could just as well be escaping the responsibilities of family life. Leisure is what these people give themselves to because it allows them to lose themselves in it and forget reality.

The second broad attitude is the rejection of leisure. This is where leisure is seen as a bad thing – usually in terms of being lazy and selfish, but sometimes bad in and of itself.

A common version of this is called utilitarianism. This is where something is evaluated only by how useful it is. Leisure activities are then thought to be intrinsically worthless and therefore not worth pursuing. The only leisure activities that are allowed are those that achieve something, such as DIY.

This approach usually gives a grudging acceptance that we cannot spend our entire life working and so time off is needed. But here's the catch – it is time off only so we can recuperate to go back to work. It's the 'pit-stop' view of leisure where it is only necessary recovery time for the real deal, which is work.

Another example of this rejection of leisure view is called asceticism. This sees any pleasurable activity as fundamentally wrong: life is to be lived without enjoyment. So ascetics deliberately avoid good food or fun activities – they live an austere (and dull) lifestyle, which pretty much rules out leisure as we are thinking of it.

Work to rest, or rest to work?

We have seen that there are two broad views on leisure today – worship it or reject it. Stated simply the first says we work to rest, whereas the second says we rest to work. Of the two today the first is far and away the most common. Our society tends to live for the weekend – 'Thank God it's Friday!' is the common cry.

However we can still find elements of the second. It used to be that someone's high status in society was shown by the vast amount of leisure time they had because they didn't have to work, whereas today we would easily think of them as a time waster. Now we think important people are always needed and always busy, rather than being people of leisure.

In the Christian world the rejection of leisure is much more common. I heard someone speaking recently who said that as a child they were taught that if something was enjoyable it must be wrong! Fun equals bad. Christians have often thought in that way because many worldly pleasures are indeed very worldly – and by that I mean sinful. And so withdrawing from them is entirely appropriate. But the result has sometimes been a total denial of pleasure. God becomes a God who wants to spoil all our fun.

Similarly some people have been brought up thinking that we ought to be productive all the time and so leisure activities that don't achieve anything are to be avoided. We are told they are a waste of precious time. Leland Ryken describes the consequences of this typical Christian approach to life:

> The legacy of utilitarianism has been permanent…the test of usefulness is applied with particular rigor by evangelical Christians. The result is a thriving work ethic and an anaemic play ethic, along with a virtual neglect of art and culture.[ii]

If that's you then you may find yourself feeling guilty about the idea of leisure. We'll need to return to this and think about how appropriate it is or isn't. But first I want us to think about two last aspects of leisure today, which we can class under poor leisure.

Poor leisure

By this I am referring to our poor quantity and quality of leisure. Let us take each in turn. Most people want more time to relax and bemoan their lack of leisure time. This is often because of the amount of time they spend at work. However this is not the sole reason, as in many cases in the West working weeks are actually shorter than they were fifty years ago. In addition most people have a number of labour saving devices in the home. But despite this we are still too busy. For some it remains the domination of their work – their hours really are long, although often more through choice than compulsion.

But even in our time off we cram more and more hobbies, sports and activities in. We try to squeeze the most out of our leisure time but then end up rushed and far from rested. Technology has a lot to answer for here: computers, digital cameras/camcorders, home entertainment systems, hard disk recorders, email and mobiles. These all provide great opportunity for communication and leisure but can also dominate time off so that it stops being relaxing.

There's a mobile phone advert I saw recently which begins with pieces of watches falling from the sky. The voiceover then speaks about time as something we cannot buy or sell; rather we have all become rich in it. It goes on: From now on we all have more time. Because with cell phones the internet is truly mobile. So you can make use of every minute of every day.

So there is it: technology claiming to give us more time in the day! In some ways that's true because checking my email on the bus home from work may save time when I get home. But it may also mean that I take my work home with me, or end up less relaxed because I feel the lure of surfing the Web when I could be truly relaxing.

Plus there's the inevitable invention of new leisure activities and the pressure to keep up with what everyone else is enjoying. All of this leads to what has been called the 'Harried Leisure Class' where we acquire more things and take on more activities but feel the increasing demands of time to actually use or do any of them.

For Christians of course there's a whole extra set of things to fit in: church, meetings, reading the Bible, prayer, serving and loving each other in the church. Some of us may fill our spare time with this and never have any true leisure time – this may go hand in hand with feeling guilty about leisure as we have already mentioned above. Others may squeeze out church things because we are too busy with our leisure – this may go hand in hand with worshipping leisure. This is why we must get a clear biblical view on leisure.

Along with this there is often poor quality of leisure. Interestingly, a survey of students recently discovered that their most common complaint was that they were bored. And they usually have the largest number of leisure activities available to them and the greatest quantity of time to do them! This boredom has often been linked to people becoming increasingly passive in their leisure. There are certainly exceptions like extreme sports, but most people relax in front of a TV. They sit back and let it wash over them.

Not that there's necessarily anything wrong with that – but purely passive leisure activities turn out to be the ones we find least refreshing. People spend evening after evening watching TV (or in the case of students often morning after morning), but end up bored. People engage less and less in what would be thought of as more demanding leisure activities – for example, reading or learning a new skill.

At the other end of the spectrum some people 'work' at their leisure. Maybe it's the constant time in the garden or the sport they train for and play endlessly. They set ambitious targets for themselves and work at them. So all their spare time is thrown into one thing; and it is often thrown in with more ambition than their working day. Now again, there's not necessarily anything wrong with really giving yourself to one hobby, but this usually results in poor quality leisure. It is not very relaxing or recuperating.

How are you resting?

How is your leisure time? How do you think about it? Do you have very much of it? What do you do with it? Is it good quality leisure? It might be helpful to ask which of the following categories you might fit into:

• I tend to feel guilty about leisure and think I should be productive all the time.

• I tend to worship leisure time and live for it.

• I tend to be happy with leisure but it's usually boring.

• I tend to try to fit too much into my leisure time and so don't actually enjoy it.

We have begun by examining leisure today and thinking of the range of attitudes and approaches we might have towards it. Crucially as Christians we need to ask what God thinks about our leisure. That's what we turn to look at next.

2

Reasons to rest

The Bible doesn't talk about leisure directly, at least not as we talk about it today. What it does talk about though is the idea of rest, and linked with that is the idea of the Sabbath. That is one day off in seven. It's a pretty simple idea in itself but unfortunately it can get complicated. We're not going to be able to delve into all the arguments surrounding rest and the Sabbath, but we do need to look at them briefly and draw out some implications for leisure today.

Rest because of creation

The creation of the world in Genesis 1 is well known – God speaks and his powerful creative word brings the physical creation into being. We need to look at what happens on the seventh day:

> *By the seventh day God had finished the work he had been doing; so on the seventh day he rested from all his work. Then God blessed the seventh day and made it holy, because on it he rested from all the work of creating that he had done.*
> *(Genesis 2:2-3)*

What did God do on the seventh day? He rested from 'all the work of creating'; he ceased all his activity of making the world. So it is not that God had a day off on Saturday and went back to work on Sunday. This isn't God's cycle of work where he has one day off in seven. Having created the world, on the seventh day God rested from that work of creating.

Clearly God continued to work in other ways – sustaining creation and ruling over it. And he has carried on doing and continues to do this, but at the same time he is also at rest, in the sense of having finished his creative work. And because of this rest God blessed that seventh day – set it apart, made it special.

This is in fact the climax of creation – at the end of the other days, all that's been made is declared 'good', but this actual day in itself is blessed and declared 'holy'. There is the sense of God delighting in his work of creation, satisfied with everything being as it is supposed to be.

This creation rest is connected later in the life of Israel with the command to observe the Sabbath day – that is, to have one in seven days off:

> *Remember the Sabbath day by keeping it holy. Six days you shall labour and do all your work, but the seventh day is a Sabbath to the <u>LORD</u> your God. On it you shall not do any work, neither you, nor your son or daughter, nor your male or female servant, nor your animals, nor any foreigner residing in your towns. For in six days the <u>LORD</u> made the heavens and the earth, the sea, and all that is in them, but he rested on the seventh day. Therefore the <u>LORD</u> blessed the Sabbath day and made it holy. (Exodus 20:8-11)*

The word 'Sabbath' comes from the word meaning 'rest'. And so the Sabbath is the day of rest. God's command in the passage above is that his people should remember the Sabbath day, which they are to do by keeping it holy. And that is done by not working. They should stop all their normal labour on that day. And the reason that is given is because God rested on the seventh day from all his work of creation.

God has clearly provided a pattern for us – work followed by rest. Work takes up more of the time, but rest has its place following work. This is the pattern of the created order God has given us.

But we can go further. God's rest follows his work of creation where he makes our world, makes us and everything that we need. And so when we rest we remember that we are created people who are given this world and all that is in it by our God. And so as we rest we enjoy God's creation – all that he has provided for us and given to us.

As you have time off consider all that you have from God: that he gives you food to eat and somewhere to live; that he gives you life and breath. Remember that all you have and do is ultimately because it is his gift to you.

Rest because of salvation

The concept of rest is much richer than only having time off though. To understand this further we need to refer back to the Genesis passage to see that God rested from creation because the world was as he wanted it to be. It was his perfect harmonious creation.

This theme of God's perfect creation is developed throughout the Old Testament. For example, the land that God's people are promised in the Old Testament is called their 'resting place' and the place where God will give them rest. The reason is that the Promised Land is the place where they will return to the perfection of living with God and all is as it should be. Or at least that is the ideal picture – it was never actually like that.

The writer to the Hebrews talks about this in chapters 3 and 4 saying that God's promise of perfect rest wasn't really going to be fulfilled in a patch of land in the Middle East. He had a much bigger and better idea in mind – the perfect rest of the new creation (Isaiah 65:17-25). That is when all will be as it should be once again. The 'rest' they enjoyed in the Promised Land was only a picture of what was to come.

How then do we enter God's rest? By believing the good news about Jesus. The writer to the Hebrews says that some people in the Old Testament didn't enter the land of rest because they didn't trust God's word of promise about entering the land and the rest he would give them there. And he says that it is the same for us in believing the promises of the gospel and the rest God offers us. So he concludes by calling us to make sure we enter that rest ourselves:

> There remains, then, a Sabbath-rest for the people of God; for those who enter God's rest also rest from their own work, just as God did from his. Let us, therefore, make every effort to enter that rest, so that no-one will perish by following their example of disobedience.
> (Hebrews 4:9-11)

Jesus is the one who brings true rest with God both now and finally in the new creation. Only when he returns will we find our rest and true home that the Old Testament rest looked forward to. That is when the perfect rest of Eden will be restored.

We have seen then that the Sabbath command to rest is not only a practical command that refers to the seventh day being one of rest; it also looks forward to the final and perfect rest for all who believe. And this idea of resting because of salvation comes when the Sabbath command is repeated in Deuteronomy 5:12-15:

> *Observe the Sabbath day by keeping it holy, as the <u>LORD</u> your God has commanded you. Six days you shall labour and do all your work, but the seventh day is a Sabbath to the <u>LORD</u> your God. On it you shall not do any work, neither you, nor your son or daughter, nor your male or female servant, nor your ox, your donkey or any of your animals, nor any foreigner residing in your towns, so that your male and female servants may rest, as you do. Remember that you were slaves in Egypt and that the <u>LORD</u> your God brought you out of there with a mighty hand and an outstretched arm. Therefore the <u>LORD</u> your God has commanded you to observe the Sabbath day.*

The Israelites are told to observe the Sabbath day by keeping it holy, which is to be done by not working. But do you see that the reason given is different this time from the one in the Exodus passage? The Israelites are to rest once a week because God rescued them from Egypt. And in fact the connection between these two things is even more obvious in the original language (Hebrew). Look at these two phrases side by side:

> *Six days you shall labour and do all your work, but the seventh day is a Sabbath to the <u>LORD</u> your God.*

> *Remember that you were labourers in Egypt and that the <u>LORD</u> your God brought you out of there. (author's own translation)*

The Israelites' working week was paralleled with their time working in Egypt, and the Sabbath day is paralleled with being rescued by God.

This fits with what we saw above. The Promised Land was the place of rest which pictures salvation. God delivers the Israelites from slavery in Egypt to bring them into a place of rest, and they are to have a day of rest to remember that.

This is why the Sabbath is such a big deal in the rest of the Old Testament. It is referred to as a sign of the covenant (Exodus 31:17). Anyone who breaks the Sabbath is to be cut off from the people of Israel, because to do that is to say to God that you don't want his salvation; it is to reject his offer of rest (see Exodus 31:14).

So we rest not only as the pattern of creation, but also to remember that God has saved us from slavery – he has saved us so that we can once again enjoy him and his creation as he intended, rather than being doomed to endless toil. We must rest to remember and anticipate the eternal rest that he has promised us. As you rest, reflect on the pleasure of relaxing and the satisfaction of work achieved, and look forward to the day of perfect rest to come.

Rest because you need to

People were also commanded to rest because they needed refreshment. This isn't the primary reason for the Sabbath command, but it is still there. The fact is that God hasn't made us to be machines that can just keep on running 24/7. We need sleep for a start. But neither has God made us to be machines that just have to go on to sleep mode every so often; we actually have to switch off from work, we need to rest.

Here is one way the Sabbath command is expressed with this need for refreshment:

> Six days do your work, but on the seventh day do not work, so that your ox and your donkey may rest and the slave born in your household, and the foreigner among you as well, may be refreshed.
> (Exodus 23:12)

That last word 'refreshed' has the idea of drawing breath – of being exhausted and then recuperating.

You see this also in the life of Jesus. In Mark we are told that so many people were coming and going that Jesus said to his disciples, 'Come with me by yourselves to a quiet place and get some rest' (Mark 6:31). And so we read that 'they went away by themselves in a boat to a solitary place' (verse 32). They needed time for rest and recuperation.

Some professional career people need to hear this – especially those beginning a career. There can be something intoxicating about working life at first. Later on in a career too, we can simply feel that there is no escape. The danger is to think that we have endless energy and resources, and can keep going. We can't, we won't. Make sure you rest; we need refreshment.

People whose work is in the home need to hear this as well. If your work involves child-care, cooking and running a house, it is very easy to do those things seven days a week because they need doing. Think back to the Old Testament laws and commands. This is why to observe the Sabbath there were commands not to light a fire to cook; you had to prepare food the day before. It is not easy to say exactly what that looks like today – we don't have to draw strict rules like that. But is there rest time for you where you are refreshed? Does your spouse give you time off some of those duties? What about for example getting a take-away once a week?

So we rest for at least three reasons:
  • Because of creation: to enjoy God's provision.
  • Because of salvation: to remember God's gift of eternal rest.
  • Because we need to: to have time for refreshment from our work.

Resting today

What does all this mean for a day of rest today? There has been endless discussion on how the command to observe the Sabbath should be interpreted today, and there are some recommended books at the end which you may find useful.

First, the command to observe the Sabbath is never repeated in the New Testament whereas the other nine of the Ten Commandments are repeated in some form or other. Some say that as the other nine are repeated, we should assume the Sabbath is as well. But it seems more likely to me that the Sabbath command is missing intentionally: its absence should alert us to something.

Secondly, we know that when there was pressure on Christians to observe certain Jewish feasts – special days or months – Paul says they are not to think they need to observe such things, because they have been fulfilled in Christ (Galatians 4:9-11; Colossians 2:16-17). So in Colossians 2 he says that Sabbath days were part of the shadow, but the reality has come in Christ.

Thirdly, there is the statement in Romans 14 where Paul is discussing Jewish issues like food laws, and he comments that some people have a conscience about certain things; some don't. And in that context, he says this:

> *Some consider one day more sacred than another; others consider every day alike. Everyone should be fully convinced in their own mind.*
> *(Romans 14:5)*

I think this indicates that Paul no longer sees the Sabbath command as applying in the same way it used to.

No to 'Sabbath', but yes to 'rest'

All that is to conclude that I don't think Christians today are commanded to have a certain day off once a week like God's people did in the Old Testament. However, there is still a clear principle of rest.

And it is this principle of rest that I think the Bible now teaches us, not the specifics. More important than the specifics are the reasons. We too should rest to enjoy God's gift of creation, to remember his gift of salvation, and to be refreshed and recuperate.

More than your average time off

What does this all mean for us in practice? It surely means that our rest has a different perspective to the rest of our culture. We look back to creation, and rejoice in the goodness of all God has given us. We remember salvation and all that God will give us in the future. And we remember we are physical beings who need to draw breath.

That means we view our rest time and leisure time differently to those around us. We should actually have a very high view of leisure. We think of it at its best as a taste of God's perfect harmony in creation, where we enjoy all that he's made in the way he intended, and as a result we are refreshed for our ongoing work.

Therefore we should be committed to leisure – committed to it as a good thing in and of itself. We should not have a utilitarian view, thinking that rest is only good so we can work more. This is the 'pit-stop' view of leisure we mentioned earlier, where we get necessary recuperation and then are back on track as quickly as possible. We certainly shouldn't hold the view that sees a day off as only time to squeeze in more work of a different sort. Rather, Christians should be those who are very positive about time off and who revel in it.

Are you resting? Why?

It's worth finishing this section with some questions for us to consider. First, we should ask whether we are resting. This won't be an issue for everyone but some people will struggle to rest. If that describes you, then think about why that is. Is there ambition or a desire to prove yourself? Is your identity bound up in what you do and how well you do it? Do you think you must squeeze as much as you can out of life or that God demands your busyness?

Not taking proper rest is a serious issue. It displays a lack of trust in God, a rejection of how he has created you and the world, and even a despising of his offer of salvation rest.

Assuming you do rest, think about the following questions and where God would want you to change your thinking:

• Do you have a high or low view of rest/leisure? Why?

• Do you rest because of how God has made you and the world, or just because it is what everyone else does?

• Does your rest ever remind you of the perfect rest God has won for you?

• What attitude do you have towards leisure time? Is it something you decide about independently or are you concerned with what God wants?

3

Can I enjoy myself?

A week or so ago I was lying on a beach in France. I had already built a huge sandcastle with my three kids (including a proper bridge over the moat that I was especially pleased with) before jumping in the breakers with my daughter; now I was relaxing. The sand was soft, the sun was warm and it felt great! But when Christians relax like this, they often feel guilty.

Closely linked with our understanding of rest and leisure is our thinking about pleasure, and if we consider pleasure as bad then our leisure time is going to suffer. For example, we may not allow much time for it, and what we do have won't be much fun if we don't think we should enjoy ourselves.

So far we have seen that we should have time to rest. Now we need to think practically about what is appropriate to do with it; in particular, whether we should and can enjoy ourselves.

God gives us things to enjoy

> Command those who are rich in this present world not to be arrogant nor to put their hope in wealth, which is so uncertain, but to put their hope in God, who richly provides us with everything for our enjoyment.
> (1 Timothy 6:17)

Here is a comment from Paul to Timothy about people who were well off. This is primarily a verse about where our trust is – is it in our wealth or is it in God? In saying we should put our hope in God Paul describes God as the one who provides for us. Notice how he puts it: he says that God provides us with everything we have, and provides for us 'richly'. And then notice that God provides these things so we can enjoy them or take pleasure in them.

So the life of hope in God is the life where we see that all we have is given generously by him and is given so that we can enjoy it. As one writer says, 'God is not a celestial scrooge who hates to see his children enjoy themselves.' Rather than that kill-joy view of God, we should have a give-joy view of God! God richly provides for our pleasure in life.

We see this idea of God giving us good things to enjoy elsewhere in the Bible as well. For example Psalm 104 says this:

> He makes grass grow for the cattle,
> and plants for people to cultivate—
> bringing forth food from the earth:
> wine that gladdens human hearts,
> oil to make their faces shine,
> and bread that sustains their hearts.
> (Psalm 104:14-15)

Notice again how God is described as the one who provides for his world. He provides food for both animals and people. But also notice that he provides wine which 'gladdens' our hearts – the word there means to make us rejoice. A good glass of wine is something to enjoy: its uplifting effect is not to be rejected; rather it is a good gift of God.

Notice also that God gives oil to make our face shine. We might not smear oil over our faces today but this is still something of an endorsement of beauty products! The psalmist is rejoicing in God's gifts that go far beyond what we need to simply live; for as he points out we have wine and oil to enhance our enjoyment of life.

Of course such good gifts can be badly abused – we will say more about that in the next chapter – but such abuse does not mean they should be rejected from the outset.

Another verse for us on this theme comes from one of Paul's speeches in Acts. He is explaining something of who God is to a group of non-Christians in the town of Lystra when he says this:

Yet he has not left himself without testimony: he has shown kindness by giving you rain from heaven and crops in their seasons; he provides you with plenty of food and fills your hearts with joy.
(Acts 14:17)

There is a similarity here to Psalm 104 – God is the one who provides us with food through a creation that produces crops, but also the one who gives us joy and gladness. God is not anti-pleasure or anti-happiness.

No super-spiritual denial

We can see this same lesson from the opposite angle. In 1 Timothy Paul is speaking to some people who were into super-spiritual denial. They argued that parts of normal life – such as marriage and certain foods – should be rejected. This is what Paul says in reply:

Such teachings come through hypocritical liars, whose consciences have been seared as with a hot iron. They forbid people to marry and order them to abstain from certain foods, which God created to be received with thanksgiving by those who believe and who know the truth. For everything God created is good, and nothing is to be rejected if it is received with thanksgiving, because it is consecrated by the word of God and prayer.
(1 Timothy 4:2-5)

We will look at this verse again in the next chapter in the context of what it teaches us about how to enjoy leisure properly. For now though just see that Paul doesn't think there's anything spiritual or worthwhile about denying yourself regular parts of creation – in this case, food and marriage. Instead, such things are to be accepted with thanksgiving to God who has given them. In fact those who say we should not enjoy such good gifts from God are 'hypocritical liars'!

And let us notice that Paul isn't talking here about only food and marriage as he broadens it to say that everything that God has made as part of creation is good, and is to be received with thanksgiving. Again, whilst we must recognize that many of God's good gifts are used wrongly this doesn't mean that they must be rejected outright.

Think about how God made the world

John Calvin, who was one of the reformers in the sixteenth century, wrote about this. He said that God made the world for our good, and that if we only looked at creation, we will see that God has designed it to be an enjoyable place to be. Here's part of what he says:

> Now then, if we consider for what end he created food, we shall find that he consulted not only for our necessity, but also for our enjoyment and delight. Thus, in clothing, the end was, in addition to necessity, comeliness and honour; and in herbs, fruits, and trees, beside their various uses, gracefulness of appearance and sweetness of smell.

> Has the Lord adorned flowers with all the beauty which spontaneously presents itself to the eye, and the sweet odour which delights the sense of smell, and shall it be unlawful for us to enjoy that beauty and this odour? What? Has he not so distinguished colours as to make some more agreeable than others? Has he not given qualities to gold and silver, ivory and marble, thereby rendering them precious above other metals or stones? In short, has he not given many things value without having any necessary use? [iii]

Do you see the argument? The way God made food, clothing, flowers and everything else is not purely functional. God could have made food that nourished us but was boring and tasteless. But instead he has made it so that we can season and flavour food in different and delightful ways. And the same goes for clothing and colours and jewels.

Notice in the last line quoted above Calvin says that God has given us many things of value that don't have any necessary use. In other words God has not created a purely functional or minimalist creation but instead an enjoyable creation.

And so we should enjoy what God has given. If he's made beautiful flowers to look at, then he wants us to contemplate them. If he's made food good to taste, he wants us to cook it well and enjoy the flavours. And we could say the same of sports and music and art and so on.

This is simply another angle on the verses above (1 Timothy 4:2-5; Psalm 104:14-15) that say God gives us things for our enjoyment. Now clearly we can get this wrong – we could end up living for good food. We will come back to that in the next chapter. But we must understand the principle first: Christians are not anti-pleasure; we think God's made a good creation with lots of good things that we can and should enjoy.

... So enjoy stuff!

This view will influence our rest. We can and should enjoy hobbies, sports, arts, craft, nature, music, history, games, social times, family times, and everything else that is a good part of this world. We are to embrace the enjoyment of God's gifts in creation. We don't despise such things as worldly or 'unspiritual'. And so we can and should seek out enjoyable ways of relaxing and recuperating.

We enjoy leisure simply as leisure. In other words, leisure is its own end. As in the last chapter, we need to emphasize once again that we should not have that utilitarian view of leisure where it is only good for what it gives us.

Of course leisure time must not be used as an excuse for avoiding other responsibilities – that is to go to the other extreme. But the point is that leisure time doesn't have to be productive as we saw in the utilitarianism view. If you happen to enjoy needlework or cutting the grass then that's great, but it's also OK not to! It's fine to watch a film, play football, read a book or go for walk, without doing them for the benefits of education or exercise that they might produce. We can and should enjoy pointless activities: pointless in terms of what they produce. They are not pointless in being an enjoyment of creation.

So often we can create a hierarchy of ways of spending our Saturday afternoon. Top of the list comes anything to do with church life or caring for others. Then comes DIY or gardening, or other productive activities. But non-productive activities are a waste of time. If we think this way, then we basically don't believe in true leisure.

So ask yourself, do you have a nagging unease when you relax, telling you to be doing something more useful? Do you feel guilty for relaxing? If you do you've slipped into this utilitarian view that rest is only good for its usefulness. And I want to encourage you to see rest as a good thing, and something to be enjoyed in and of itself.

Work at enjoying leisure

This might sound like a contradiction – especially in the light of what I have just said. What I mean here is that the Christian view of rest sees that it's something to be embraced and enjoyed. By contrast our culture often has a 'passing the time' view of leisure. We do things to distract ourselves, until we have to go back to work. More and more our culture has an approach that says 'entertain me', while expecting to sit back and not engage ourselves.

For many people this often means hours watching TV; for others it might be surfing the net, or playing computer games. Not that there is anything wrong with that – I enjoy TV a great deal; it's a good way to relax. But it's easy for us to slide into only those passive forms of rest. I don't think that fits with the positive view the Bible gives us of what God provides us with. The passive only idea of leisure misses the concept of enjoying all of God's good gifts.

Put differently, think of how God has created us with our imaginations, minds, physical bodies, coordination, artistic talents, and so on. I don't think a passive approach to leisure captures all that we are. It becomes a monochrome view of what can and should be multicolour. Again I want to say that there's nothing wrong with sitting in front of the TV, but I also want to say that some of us need to get out more, do an evening class, pick a hobby, socialize, take up a sport, visit a museum, or go for a walk. Do leisure activities that reflect all that God has made us to be and the world he has given us.

I must emphasize that this is an area that varies between people greatly. I remember once being taken to the opera by a friend (the one and only time I have ever been); they thought it was a wonderful way to spend an evening; I thought it was sheer tedium – I would have left early if I could! So one person's enjoyable leisure can be someone else's nightmare. We must not legislate for each other in this.

But many of us slide towards only passive leisure activities. The irony is that many more active leisure times are actually more relaxing and refreshing. That's what I mean by working at leisure to enjoy it.

Make the most of now?

There is an advertising group whose tag line in all their adverts says – 'make the most of now'. The adverts focus on squeezing as much enjoyment and satisfaction out of life as we can. It is an alluring line which appeals to us to get the most out of life.

So is this what I am saying: God gives us good things for our enjoyment so we should just throw ourselves into enjoying life? I think the answer is 'yes' and 'no'.

It is 'yes' in that we have seen that God wants us to enjoy his good gifts in creation – he gives them for our joy. Many Christians need to hear that – there is within many of us a lurking suspicion that fun is bad in God's eyes. We need to embrace this truth that we can enjoy these good gifts, and that will be shown in our leisure.

But the answer is also 'no', as we don't just throw ourselves into this life; for the Christian, life embraces so much more. The world's take on this is that you only live once, so why not make the most of life by having the most fun and pleasure possible? We see this in the lists of the top 100 things to do or places to visit before you die.

The Christian knows there is far more to this life and that there is another life to come. That means enjoying life takes its place in a much bigger picture – it must not be all we live for. We all need to be reminded of this – we can sometimes be identical to the world around us in our approach to pleasure, just out to get as much from it as we can.

Christians should embrace the pleasures of life and make the most of them – but we do so as those who know they come from God. Knowing God is the source of our pleasure changes our view of things completely. We thank him for it and look to enjoy leisure as he would want us to, rather than throwing ourselves into it just because it's fun. We also know that this same God calls us to sacrifice and service; we know there is more to life than pleasure. We will think more about that change of attitude in the next chapter.

Do you enjoy leisure?

Again some questions for you to consider:

• Do you feel guilty about non-productive leisure time? If so how do you think God wants you to change your thinking?

• Do you think of enjoyment as something God gives, or something you find for yourself? What difference does that make?

• What leisure activities do you have? Are they mainly passive or active? What might you want to change?

• Do you slip into living for pleasure and making the most of life as the world around does? How should the bigger perspectives of the Christian life change that?

4

Life with leisure

We have seen that rest and leisure is a good part of how God has made the world and that we should rest and should enjoy creation. In this last chapter we will think through how we go about this life with leisure.

Glorifying God in our leisure

Paul says to the Corinthian church, 'whether you eat or drink or whatever you do, do it all for the glory of God' (1 Corinthians 10:31). All of life, with whatever is done in it, is to be done glorifying God. So how do we glorify God with our leisure?

Give thanks for leisure

There are two key elements. First we must thank God for it. Let's look back at a few comments from Paul that we saw in the last chapter – it's where he's responding to people who want to deny enjoying good parts of creation.

> Such teachings come through hypocritical liars, whose consciences have been seared as with a hot iron. They forbid people to marry and order them to abstain from certain foods, which God created to be received with thanksgiving by those who believe and who know the truth. For everything God created is good, and nothing is to be rejected if it is received with thanksgiving, because it is consecrated by the word of God and prayer.
> (1 Timothy 4:2-5)

We saw that this super-spiritual denial of good things in creation is actually poisonous false teaching. But we can also see here how we should approach God's gifts to us in creation and so glorify him. We should receive them 'with thanksgiving'. It is so important that Paul says it twice!

The explanation of this comes in the last phrase: 'because it is consecrated by the word of God and prayer.' The word 'consecrated' here simply means that it is declared OK – good or right for us. And God's good gifts to us are 'right for us' because of two things.

First, there's God's word to us about them – that is he has said that things like food are his good gifts and so he has given his endorsement on them. Second, they are also right for us because of prayer. Prayer expresses something about our receiving them. I think this must be a prayer of thanks; it is how we receive things with thanksgiving.

And so the question that arises is: 'Do I pray prayers of thanks over my leisure activities?' G.K. Chesterton put this well in saying that while others said 'grace' before meals, he said grace before reading a book, painting or walking. Do we express our thanks to God over a day in the garden, an evening watching a film, a drink with friends?

Thanking God in this way changes our perspective completely. When we thank someone we think of what we have received as a gift: we are glad for it and appreciative to the giver. So if I enjoy playing football and God is the one who has given us sport and physical abilities, then as I play football I am glad for it and thank God for it. That gives him glory for his generosity and goodness.

And the same is true if I enjoy cooking or knitting or films or books – or whatever. I thank God for his good gifts. That attitude is very different to that of our culture. Most people simply think that whatever they enjoy in recreation just happens to be part of the world around us. And so they may consider themselves lucky to have such enjoyment, or may think they deserve it, or think they have created it and made it for themselves. All of which are very different to being given it.

Use leisure as God wants

The second aspect of glorifying God in our leisure is in using it as he wants. That is going about it in the way he would want me to. So if he has given us food as a good gift that we should receive with thanksgiving, we must use food in the way God wants us to – for example, by not being greedy. If he has given us wine to gladden our hearts, we must 'use' it in the way he intends – enjoying its taste and uplifting effect and thanking him for it, but being aware of drunkenness or a dependence on needing a drink.

We know that sin will work its way in and through every part of life, and so we should be on guard in our leisure as much as anywhere else. We can begin with the easy stuff: we know some leisure activities are wrong. We should not get drunk, take drugs, watch dodgy films and so on. That is where the activity itself is sinful. We must stand apart from all such 'leisure' as a misuse of God's good gifts in creation.

But what about when the activity itself is fine? There's nothing wrong with sport or painting or reading. How will our sin show itself there? It can (and will) happen in a variety of ways. J.I. Packer says that the motive behind our pursuit of leisure is key. He says that if we are preoccupied with ourselves and not with God we will turn a good activity into a worldly rather than godly pursuit. This might be because we focus on ourselves and our enjoyment; it might be because we approach leisure as our right; fundamentally it will be because we ignore God. So whether it's playing football or enjoying a meal, the same leisure activity can be done well or badly all depending on the attitudes of our heart. As a result good leisure activities can be done very wrongly – it all depends on the way in which they are handled.[iv]

The fact is our leisure time can be the place we can be most self-centred, proud, jealous or unkind. People's attitude on the sports field can be shocking when their competitiveness starts to override any concern for those around them. A superiority complex over others in your pottery class or snide comments about others' efforts is disgraceful. A concern with ourselves and how much fun we are having rather than a concern for others reveals a very selfish heart.

We must be those who display 'compassion, kindness, humility, gentleness and patience' (Colossians 3:12). We must be those who want to serve others around us and so look to their interests rather than our own (Philippians 2:3-4). We want to be those who rid ourselves of all anger and malice

(Colossians 3:8). And these attitudes must be shown in our leisure just as much as anywhere else in the Christian life.

I play five-a-side football on Monday evenings. I'm very aware of the potential for pride (mainly because I'm deluded rather than any good at football!) and competitiveness that results in rash challenges and looking down on others' mistakes. I try to pray before I play and simply ask God to help me glorify him on Monday evenings. But the same should be true for the great cook preparing food, who is aware of how their head might swell as compliments are made about the food.

One friend I used to play football with found some of these sorts of issues such a problem (he was actually very good at football and was aware of his pride) he thought it best not to play. The activity was fine in itself but raised such issues of godliness for him that it was better not to do it.

What attitudes do you need to beware of in your leisure? What should you pray for? Is there anything you should stop doing, either because it is wrong in itself or because you cannot control yourself (whether thoughts or actions) when doing it?

Caution: beware of worshipping leisure

Some of us may need to be challenged to rest more and have a higher view of rest and leisure – I hope that reading this has done that. But we must also say that many of us need to be challenged not to worship rest and leisure. We said at the start that this was the main attitude our culture offers today. If people don't live for their work they live for their weekend and its entertainments. There is the possibility for your life to orientate around particular leisure activities or a 'leisure-lifestyle'.

Adverts tell us that self-gratification and seeking whatever is most relaxing and fun for me is all OK. We are constantly told that if only we buy this or do that we'll enjoy life more. Along with that we will feel the pressure of those around us. Whether it is the leisure activities of the cool teenager or student, the 20s singles, young couples, or the middle-aged family, we know what is expected as 'normal' leisure. We feel the pressure to conform.

The challenge for us is not to reject leisure itself but to beware of becoming those who are 'lovers of pleasure rather than lovers of God' (2 Timothy 3:4).

So where is the line between enjoying something properly and worshipping it? There are two key questions to ask ourselves. One is: 'Can I live without this?' When we worship something it dominates life and we cannot see how we could go without it – or we live thinking that life would only be OK, or would be so much better, if we were able to have or do whatever it may be.

So we have to ask ourselves whether we can live without football, good coffee, fun holidays, TV, etc. That's not to say we wouldn't miss them – but the question gets to the core, to how much we are in their grip, and what degree of control these things have over us (which always happens when we worship something). Just asking the question and seeing what emotional reaction we have gives a pretty good indication.

The second question is: 'Do I give thanks for this?' Do you remember the importance of thanksgiving in the quote from 1 Timothy above? We said there that giving thanks was a key element in glorifying God in our leisure. It is also a key element in not worshipping our leisure.

Do we say thank you for sport, recipes, literature, music, gardens, or whatever we consider our leisure? If we do, then we keep it in its place. It's part of creation, and we can thank the creator for it. As a result we may enjoy it a great deal but we are worshipping him not it. But if we are not thankful to God for what he gives us, we may be bowing down to the god of leisure and pleasure.

An example of caution in leisure

Once again the reformer John Calvin gives good guidance in the caution we should approach leisure. We quoted from him earlier where he said that the way God had created the world showed us we ought to enjoy it. But he goes on to tell us how to be cautious so that we do not sin in that enjoyment:

> First one restraint is imposed when we hold that the object of creating all things was to teach us to know their author, and feel grateful for his

indulgence. Where is the gratitude if you so gorge or stupify yourself with feasting and wine as to be unfit for offices of piety, or the duties of your calling?

Where is the thankfulness to God for clothing, if on account of sumptuous raiment we both admire ourselves and disdain others? Or if, from a love of show and splendour, we pave the way for immodesty? Where is our recognition of God, if the glare of these things captivates our minds?

For many are so devoted to luxury in all their senses that their mind lies buried: many are so delighted with marble, gold, and pictures, that they become marble-hearted – are changed as it were into metal, and made like painted figures. The kitchen with its savoury smells so engrosses them that they have no spiritual savour.[v]

Calvin points out the cautions we have already mentioned. We must beware of the way enjoying creation can tempt us to sinful attitudes. He gives the example of clothing: there's nothing wrong with enjoying fashion and nice clothes, but not if it means we admire ourselves and look down on others, and not if it results in immodesty.

And more generally we must always see them as gifts from God that we thank him for. I love his phrase 'Where is our recognition of God, if the glare of these things captivates our minds?' We can fall into worship of leisure where our thinking is captivated by it; at this point we have ceased to recognize that God gives us these good things for us to enjoy.

Remembering the total gospel life

To return to the rest–work spectrum we mentioned at the beginning, we must remind ourselves that rest is only one part of the equation; the other is work. We must remember that rest only makes sense in relationship to work – rest is rest from work. And so the issue for us is not only having a good understanding of rest and leisure, but a good understanding of work as well. Otherwise we will always tend to live for one and despise the other. A high view of rest should never be used to justify idleness which the Bible sees as a sinful shirking of our responsibilities (Proverbs 26:14-15; 2 Thessalonians 3:10-12).

As well as work we must remember other responsibilities God gives us and calls us to, including family life, friends and church. That means this high view of leisure we've been speaking about finds its place within the total life lived for God. A positive approach to leisure must never be used to justify a lack of responsibility elsewhere.

This does, I know, lead to the juggling of time and responsibilities. But God knows how many hours are in the day and doesn't expect us to squeeze in more. He simply calls us to make wise and godly decisions about how to use the time he has given us and to be content to achieve whatever is done in that time.

The Christian then may decide not to go for certain leisure activities because of their impact on the rest of life. They may simply be too time-consuming or they may conflict unhelpfully with family life or have a negative impact on their involvement with the church community. The Christian in fact will happily make sacrifices over their leisure time for the sake of others, while still having a positive view of leisure.

So how much do I rest?

This is such a difficult area to be specific. We must recognize that we are different to each other in several ways. We are all wired differently – some of us can do with less sleep and still have bundles of energy, while others of us are terrible without a solid eight hours a night. That is not an issue of godliness of spirituality – it's our physical make up.

We also vary in life situations – some will be younger with more energy than those who are older; some will be single and with fewer responsibilities than those who are married; some will have young children and be exhausted, others will not or will have older children who are a different drain on their time. All this simply means we shouldn't expect to look at someone else and rest in the way they do; and we must all beware of making our pattern of rest the pattern for others.

Having said that we must repeat that laziness is wrong and some of us will be tempted into it; just as overwork is wrong and some of us will be tempted into that. Some questions worth asking ourselves are:

• Does my conscience condemn me? Do I feel uneasy about how much or how little rest I have? I must be careful here because my conscience can be wrong – it can especially be affected by my background, but it's still worth asking the question.

• What do other people think? That might be my spouse, my friends, my home group, my church leaders. Talk to each other about this and be prepared to ask people for their honest opinion. If we are considering taking up a new hobby or career change let's run it past others for their advice first rather than only ever making such decisions by ourselves.

• Are there responsibilities I have that I either don't do or don't do well because of my rest? In other words are my leisure choices having a negative impact elsewhere in life? Rest should help me recuperate so I can live the rest of life well; not overtake my time or thinking so that I don't do my work or care for my family or live within the church community as I should.

Conclusion

So where does this all leave us? How will this affect the time you spend at home in the evenings or on a Saturday afternoon?

We have seen that we have been made to work, and to rest, and to play. There is to be a balance that is to be found in these which each of us must find for ourselves. What I hope that you will take away from this book is not a one-answer-fits-all solution, but a number of principles that you can apply to your particular situation.

We all face the possibility of getting the balance wrong – in what we do, how much we do, and how we do it. Praise God that he bears with us and forgives us. But do consider your rest and leisure and think through how Jesus will be Lord of it. Think through how you do it and how you will glorify him in it. Beware of excusing subtle sins within it and see what changes you can and should make. Do that now whilst these things are still fresh in your mind!

Remember every moment of every day is claimed by God and counter claimed by Satan. Let us live all of our lives under Jesus as Lord, by the power of the Holy Spirit and for the glory of God. And let us long for the day when we will finally be at rest with God.

Notes

i C.S. Lewis, *Christian Reflections*, edited by Walter Hooper (Grand Rapids, MI: Eerdmans, 1967), p. 33.

ii Leland Ryken, *Work and Leisure in Christian Perspective* (Leicester: IVP, 1990), p. 82.

iii John Calvin, *Institutes of the Christian Religion*, trans. Henry Beveridge (Grand Rapids, MI: Eerdmans, 1964), p. 32.

iv See J.I. Packer, '*Leisure and Life-Style: Leisure, Pleasure and Treasure*', in God and Culture, edited by D.A. Carson and John D. Woodbridge (Grand Rapids, MI: Eerdmans, 1993), p. 365.

v John Calvin, *Institutes of the Christian Religion*, p. 33.

Further reading

Beynon, Graham, *Jesus@Work* (Belfast: 10Publishing, 2008)

Chester, Tim, *The Busy Christian's Guide to Busyness* (Leicester: IVP, 2006)

Hardyman, Julian, *Glory Days: Living the Whole of Your Life for Jesus* (Leicester: IVP, 2006)

Ryken, Leland, *Work and Leisure in Christian Perspective* (Leicester: IVP, 1990)

These books are available via **www.10ofthose.com**